CW00486435

Air Fryer
Cookbook

Fry, Bake, Grill & Roast Healthy & Low Carb
Irresistible Dishes

GILLIAN HINES

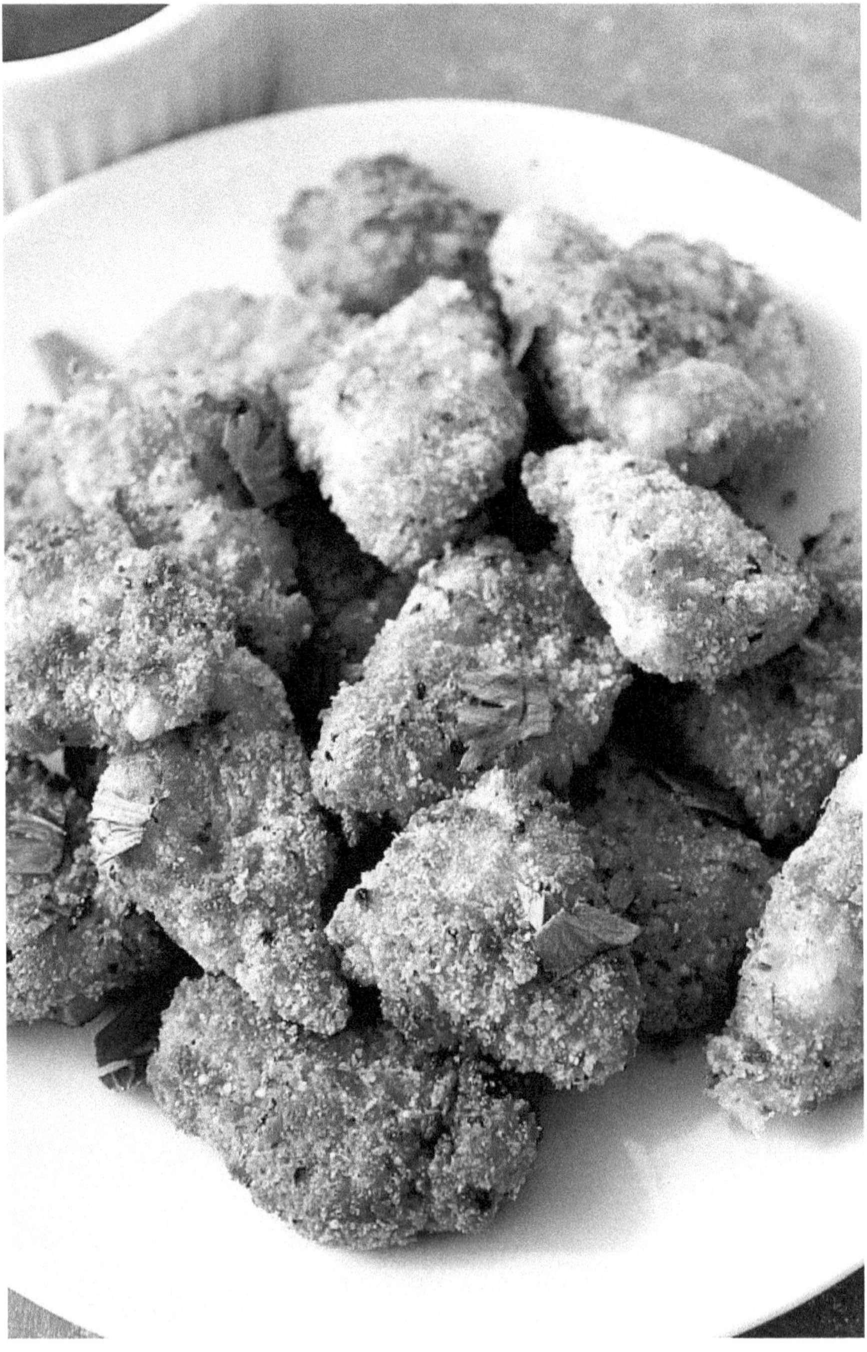

Table of content

The trademarks used are without any consent, and the publication of the trademark is without permission or backing by the trademark owner. All trademarks and brands within this book are for clarifying purposes only and are owned by the owners themselves, not affiliated with this document.

Introduction

An air fryer is the most sought-after appliance as of its versatility and usage. The Air Fryer can cook food by circulating hot air through the cooking chamber. It is a kitchen gadget that can revolutionize the way you cook, makes your cooking quick and easy. It's a sophisticated and more advanced edition of the old traditional fryers and ovens.

The vortex fan makes it possible for the air fryer to circulate hot air within the Fryer's chamber, making the cooking process faster and without consuming much oil. The microprocessor technology utilized in the appliance makes the cooking better because of the programmed keys.

You can easily prepare your food without worrying about time or temperature. The Air Fryer is a multicooker kitchen appliance with built-in programming. This means your Fryer will fry, bake, roast, reheat, and rehydrate food. It is one of the best replacement for the traditional oven and grill, toaster and dehydrator. Since it is small, it can save a lot of space in your kitchen.

One of the most important advantages of the Air Fryer is that its increased capacity for air frying allows you to cook a large quantity of food at once.

It's exceptionally good because it saves nearly 80% of your oil when frying your food. If you want to make French fries, you'll need a small amount of oil.

It's not only good for crunchy foods, but it's still great for cooking a wide variety of foods. You can bake muffins, roast chicken, dehydrate fruits and reheat frozen foods.

The air fryer is vital since it reduces excess calories, which are also associated with weight gain. The device is designed to ensure that you get high-quality food without having to consume more calories. The food crunchiness from the outside and tender makes it different from the rest of the air fryers.

From fresh to frozen, crisped to perfect and exquisitely guilt-free, the Air Fryer allows you to make healthy versions of all your preferred fried foods. Get the same texture and flavor as deep-fried using up to 95% lower oil and enjoy quick cleanup since less oil means less mess.

The air fryer uses circulating air that is super-heated instead of hot oil to provide the same toasted flavor and texture as deep-fried cuisines. It still holds juices within the crispy covering, except without the extra oil: it's easier, healthier, cleaner, and faster.

Benefits of the Air Fryer

Since its market launch, the Air Fryer has established a lot of interest. There is a lot to like about these appliances. If you are still unaware of its advantages, here are a few that you cannot overlook.

- Without the unhealthy calories, the machine will prepare nutritious and tasty meals that resemble those cooked in oil.

- If you're quite busy with your daily routine and can't seem to make time to prepare, or if you're trying to lose weight but aren't sure how to avoid eating fried foods, an air fryer would come in handy. The delightful low-fat meals can be prepared in a flash.

- People who want a stress-free experience and dislike the cleanup phase more than the activity itself would enjoy this. This appliance is simple to clean. There will be no more scrubbing, brushing, or laboring in the kitchen.

- The air fryer's hot-air ventilation cooks food from all sides without using any oil.

- This product is among the most cost-effective on the market. When you purchase an air fryer, you'll save a lot of money, and it offers the advantages of an oven, a fryer, and a cooker. There's no infuriating smell of fried foods in the kitchen when you prepare food in an air fryer. You can eat balanced fried foods that are free of oil and smell.

- Whether you choose to grill, roast, bake, fry, or cook, an air fryer can do everything.

Cooking Tips

- One of the most important levels of food preparation is preheating. Before placing food in the cooking chamber, wait for the Display to indicate **Add Food**.

- As the Display indicates, food should be turned, flipped or rotated accordingly to ensure even cooking.

- When preparing coated foods, use breadcrumb batter rather than liquid batter to ensure that the batter adheres to the food.

- Spray food products with oil before seasoning to make sure seasoning clings to them.

- Before putting fresh potato sticks in the Air Fryer, soak them for 15 minutes in ice water, pat them dry, and gently spray them with cooking oil.

- To protect the tops of cakes, pies, quiches, and other similar items from overcooking, use a baking dish that is oven safe and filled with foil and cover it with an oven-safe lid.

- To avoid extra steam and splatter, pat moist foodstuffs dry before cooking.

- Air frying may cause food to drip oil and fat. Throughout the cooking process, gently remove and drain the Air Fryer Basket to avoid unnecessary smoke.

Chapter 1: Breakfast Recipes

Breakfast Muffins

- **Servings:** 4 / **Prep Time:** 5 minutes / **Cook Time:** 10 min
- **Difficulty level:** Easy

Ingredients:

- ¼ cup of mashed banana
- 1 cup of flour
- ¼ cup of powdered sugar
- 1 tsp. of chopped walnuts
- 1 tsp. of milk
- ½ tsp. of baking powder
- ¼ cup of butter, room temperature
- ¼ cup of oats

Directions:

1. Set the air fryer to the temperature of 320° F.

2. In a mixing bowl, combine the walnuts, sugar, butter, and banana.

3. Mix the baking powder, flour, and oats in a separate bowl.

4. Stir together the two mixtures and add milk.

5. Pour the mixture into a muffin pan that has been greased. Bake for 10 minutes in your air fryer and serve it.

Flaxseed Porridge

- **Servings:** 4 / **Prep Time:** 5 min / **Cook Time:** 5 min
- **Difficulty level:** Easy

Ingredients:
- *4 tbsp. of honey*
- *2 cups of steel-cut oats*
- *1 tbsp. of butter*
- *1 cup of flax seeds*
- *4 cups of milk*
- *1 tbsp. of peanut butter*

Directions:

1. Combine all ingredients in an ovenproof dish/pan.

2. Set an air fryer to 390° F temperature and cook for 5 minutes in an air fryer.

3. Swirl and serve it with the desired topping.

4. Enjoy.

Onion and Cheese Omelet

- **Servings:** 1 / **Prep Time:** 5 min / **Cook Time:** 8-10 min
- **Difficulty level:** Easy

Ingredients:

- *1 tbsp. olive oil*
- *2 eggs*
- *½ onion, sliced.*
- *2 tbsp. Grated cheddar cheese*
- *¼ tsp. pepper*
- *1 tsp. soy sauce*

Directions:

1. Whisk together the eggs, pepper, and soy sauce in a mixing bowl.

2. Set the air fryer to the temperature of 350°F.

3. Heat the olive oil; add onion and egg mixture to the tray/pan, and place it in an air fryer.

4. Cook for 8 to 10 minutes.

5. Serve with grated cheddar cheese on top.

Toasted Herb and Garlic Bagel

- **Servings:** 1 / **Prep Time:** 4 min / **Cook Time:** 6 min
- **Difficulty level:** Easy

Ingredients:

- *1 tbsp. of Parmesan cheese*
- *1 bagel*
- *2 tbsp. Of butter, softened*
- *Salt and pepper, to taste*
- *1 tsp. of dried basil*
- *1 tsp. of garlic powder*
- *1 tsp. of dried parsley*

Directions:

1. Preheat the air fryer to 370°F.

2. Slice the bagel in half.

3. Cook for three minutes in an air fryer.

4. In a shallow bowl, mix the Parmesan, butter, garlic, parsley, and basil.

5. Season to taste with salt and pepper.

6. Place the mixture on the toasted bagel and spread it out evenly.

7. Place the bagel back in the air fryer and cook for another 3 minutes.

Prosciutto, Mozzarella and Egg

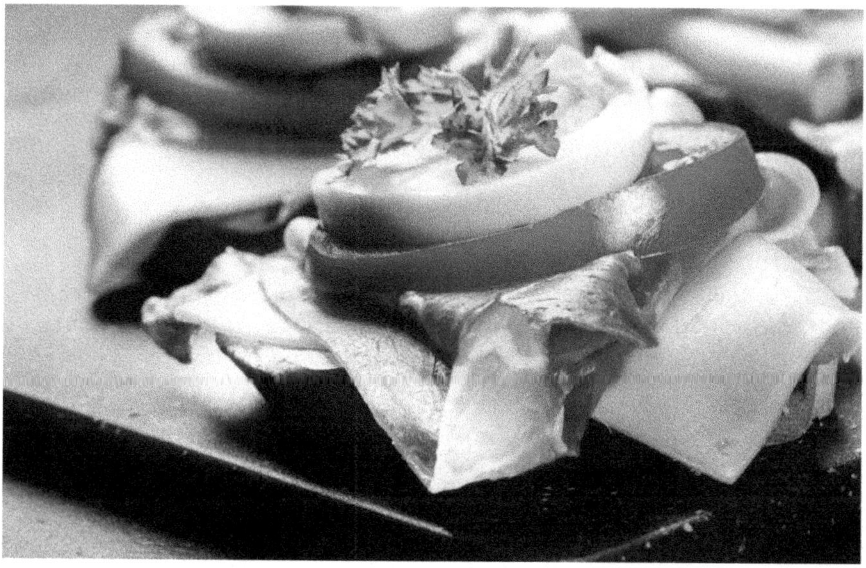

- **Servings:** 2 / **Prep Time:** 10 min / **Cook Time:** 10 min
- **Difficulty level:** Easy

Ingredients:

- *Four tomato slices*
- *2 slices of bread*
- *¼ tsp. of balsamic vinegar*
- *2 prosciutto slices, chopped*
- *¼ tsp. of maple syrup*
- *2 eggs*
- *Salt and pepper, to taste*
- *2 tbsp. grated mozzarella*
- *Cooking spray or butter for greasing*
- *2 tbsp. of mayonnaise*

Directions:

1. Set an air fryer to 320° F temperature.

2. Grease two large ramekins with cooking spray.

3. In the base of each ramekin, place one slice of bread.

4. Place two tomato slices on top of each slice of bread.

5. Evenly distribute the mozzarella among the ramekins.

6. Scatter the eggs on top of the mozzarella.

7. Drizzle with balsamic vinegar and maple syrup. Season to taste with salt and pepper.

8. Cook for 10 minutes or until the desired result is achieved.

9. Drizzle mayonnaise on top. Enjoy.

Three Meat Cheesy Omelet

✳✳✳✳✳

- **Servings:** 2 / **Prep Time:** 5 min / **Cook Time:** 12 min
- **Difficulty level:** Easy

Ingredients:

- *1 beef sausage, chopped*
- *4 slices prosciutto, chopped*
- *1 tbsp. chopped onion*
- *3 oz. Salami, chopped*
- *1 tbsp. ketchup*
- *Four eggs*
- *1 cup grated mozzarella cheese*

Directions:

1. To 350°F temperature, preheat an air fryer.

2. Mix ketchup and eggs in a mixing bowl.

3. Add the onion and mix well.

4. In the air fryer, brown the sausage for about 2 minutes.

5. Combine egg mixture, mozzarella cheese, salami, and prosciutto in a separate dish.

6. Pour this egg mixture over the sausage and stir it together.

7. Cook for about 10 minutes.

Shirred Eggs

*****

- **Servings:** 2 / **Prep Time:** 5 min / **Cook Time:** 14 min
- **Difficulty level:** Easy

Ingredients:
- *Four eggs, divided*
- *2 tsp. butter, for greasing*
- *Four slices of ham*
- *2 tbsp. Heavy cream*
- *¼ tsp. pepper*
- *3 tbsp. Parmesan cheese*
- *¼ tsp. paprika*
- *2 tsp. Chopped chives*
- *¾ tsp. salt*

Directions:

1. Set the air fryer to a temperature of 320° F.

2. Grease the butter on a pie pan. Arrange the ham slices on the pan's bottom to cover it fully. If necessary, add more slices (or less if your pan is smaller).

3. In a small shallow bowl, mix one egg, heavy cream, salt, and pepper. Drizzle the mixture over the ham slices. Scatter the remaining eggs on top of the ham. Grate the Parmesan cheese on top. Cook for 14 minutes.

4. Garnish with paprika and chives, if desired. Serve with a piece of toast. Enjoy.

Grilled Cheese Sandwich

*****

- **Servings:** 1 / **Prep Time:** 2 min / **Cook Time:** 8 min
- **Difficulty level:** Easy

Ingredients:
- *Three slices of American cheese*
- *2 slices of bread*
- *2 tsp. butter*

Directions:

1. Set an air fryer to 370° F temperature.

2. Coat the outsides of the bread with one tsp of butter.

3. Place a slice of cheese inside bread slices.

4. Place the other slice on top.

5. Cook for 4 minutes in an air fryer.

6. Toast the other side of the sandwich for another 4 minutes.

7. Slice diagonally and serve.

Chapter 2: Lunch Recipes

Grilled Apple and Brie Sandwich

*****

- **Servings:** 1 / **Prep Time:** 3 min / **Cook Time:** 5 min
- **Difficulty level:** Easy

Ingredients:
- *½ apple, thinly sliced*
- *2 bread slices*
- *2 oz. Brie cheese thinly sliced*
- *2 tsp. of butter*

Directions:

1. Heat an air fryer to 350°F.

2. Brush the outside of the bread slices with butter.

3. Place the apple and brie slices on a bread slice.

4. Cover with another slice of bread.

5. Cook for 5 minutes in an air fryer basket at 350°F.

6. Split diagonally and serve it.

Leftover Turkey and Mushroom Sandwich

*****

- **Servings:** 1 / **Prep Time:** 5 min / **Cook Time:** 9 min
- **Difficulty level:** Easy

Ingredients:
- *1 tbsp. of butter, divided*
- *½ tsp. of red pepper flakes*
- *1/3 cups of sliced mushrooms*
- *2 tomato slices*
- *¼ tsp. of salt*
- *1 hamburger bun*
- *¼ tsp. of black pepper*
- *1/3 cup of leftover turkey; shredded*

Directions:

1. Set an air fryer to the temperature of 350°F.

2. Melt half of the butter and toss in the mushrooms.

3. Cook for approximately 4 minutes.

4. In the meantime, split the bun in half and spread the leftover butter on the outside.

5. Place the turkey, mushroom, and tomato slices on it. Season with red pepper flakes and salt to taste.

6. Place the other half of the bun on top.Cook for 5 minutes and serve it.

Garlicky Chicken on Green Bed

*****

- **Servings:** 1 / **Prep Time:** 6 min / **Cook Time:** 14 min
- **Difficulty level:** Easy

Ingredients:

- *3 large kale leaves, chopped*
- *½ cup shredded romaine*
- *3 tbsp. of olive oil, divided*
- *½ cup baby spinach leaves*
- *Chicken breasts cut into cubes*
- *1 tsp. of balsamic vinegar*
- *Salt and pepper, to taste*
- *1 garlic clove, minced*

Directions:

1. Set the air fryer to 390°F.

2. Mix chicken, 1 tablespoon olive oil, and the garlic in a mixing bowl.

3. Add a pinch of salt and pepper.

4. Assemble it on a baking tray/pan lined with parchment paper; place it in an air fryer basket and cook for 14 minutes.

5. In the meantime, put the greens in a wide mixing dish.

6. Add balsamic vinegar and remaining olive oil.

7. Season it with pepper and salt.

8. Serve by placing the chicken on top.

Crispy Prosciutto and Feta Quinoa Salad

☆☆☆☆☆

- **Servings:** 2 / **Prep Time:** 5 min / **Cook Time:** 6 min
- **Difficulty level:** Moderate

Ingredients:

- ½ cup of crumbled feta cheese
- 2 prosciutto slices, chopped
- ¼ cup of chopped olives
- 1 cup of cooked quinoa
- 1 tsp. of olive oil
- Salt & pepper, to taste
- ½ red bell pepper; chopped

Directions:

1. The air fryer is preheated to 350 °F.

2. Cook for 2 minutes with olive oil and pepper.

3. Cook for 3 minutes more after adding the prosciutto.

4. Meanwhile, in an oven-proof dish, mix the feta, quinoa, and olives.

5. Season with pepper and salt and add cooked prosciutto and peppers.

6. Place the oven-proof bowl in the air fryer's basket and cook for 1 minute and serve it.

Italian Sausage Patties

- **Servings:** 4 / **Prep Time:** 7 min / **Cook Time:** 15 min
- **Difficulty level:** Easy

Ingredients:

- *¼ cup of breadcrumbs*
- *1 lb. Italian ground sausage*
- *1 tsp. of dried parsley*
- *½ tsp. of salt*
- *1 tsp. of red pepper Flakes*
- *¼ tsp. of black pepper*
- *1 egg, beaten*
- *¼ tsp. of garlic powder*

Directions:

1. Set an air fryer to 350 °F.

2. In a wide mixing bowl, combine all ingredients.

3. Line a baking sheet with parchment paper.

4. Make patties and place them on the baking sheet.

5. Cook for about 15 minutes in an air fryer.

6. Serve with tzatziki sauce.

Taquitos

*****

- **Servings:** 10/ **Prep Time:** 10 min / **Cook Time:** 13 min
- **Difficulty level:** Moderate

Ingredients:

- *1/2 cup of dry breadcrumbs*
- *2 large eggs*
- *3 tablespoons taco seasoning*
- *Ten corn tortillas (6 inches), warmed*
- *1 pound ground beef (90% lean)*
- *Optional: Salsa and guacamole*
- *Cooking spray*

Directions:

1. Preheat an air fryer to a temperature of 350°F.

2. Mix eggs, taco seasoning, and breadcrumbs in a wide mixing dish. Add the beef and stir briefly but fully.

3. In the middle of each tortilla, place 1/4 cup of beef mixture.

4. Tightly roll up and lock with toothpicks. Assemble taquitos in a layer on a greased tray in the air-fryer basket in batches; spritz with cooking spray.

5. For about 6 minutes, cook it, then turn it and cook for another 6-7 minutes, just until the meat is cooked and the taquitos are golden and crispy.

6. Before serving, remove toothpicks. Serve with guacamole and salsa, if desired.

Roasted Vegetable Salad

- **Servings:** 1 / **Prep Time:** 10 min / **Cook Time:** 20 min
- **Difficulty level:** Moderate

Ingredients:

- *Juice of 1 lemon*
- *1 potato peeled and chopped*
- *¼ tsp. of sea salt*
- *1 carrot sliced diagonally*
- *¼ onion, sliced*
- *½ small beetroot, sliced*
- *A handful of rocket salad*
- *1 cup of cherry tomatoes*
- *A handful of baby spinach*
- *½ tsp. of turmeric*
- *Parmesan shavings*
- *3 tbsp. of canned chickpeas*
- *2 tbsp. of olive oil*
- *½ tsp. of cumin*

Directions:

1. Set the air fryer to 370°F.

2. In a wide mixing dish, combine the potato, onion, cherry tomatoes, beetroot, carrot, cumin, turmeric, sea salt, and 1 tablespoon olive oil. Place this mixture in the air fryer and for 20 minutes cook it. Set aside for 2 minutes to cool.

3. In a serving dish, combine the rocket salad, lemon juice, spinach and 1 tablespoon olive oil. Combine ingredients in a mixing bowl.

4. Toss in the cooked vegetables. Sprinkle with Parmesan shavings and chickpeas before serving.

Chapter 3: Side Dishes & Snacks

Buttermilk Onion Rings

- **Servings:** 4 / **Prep Time:** 5 min / **Cook Time:** 8-12 min
- **Difficulty level:** Easy

Ingredients:

- *1 package cornbread mix*
- *2 sweet onions*
- *1 tsp. of salt*
- *2 cups of buttermilk*
- *2 cups of water*
- *2 cups of pancake mix*

Directions:

1. Preheat an air fryer to 370°F.

2. Cut the onions into rings.

3. Combine water and the pancake mix in a mixing bowl.

4. Line a baking sheet with parchment paper.

5. Dip the rings first in the cornbread mix, then in buttermilk and finally coat it with the pancake batter.

6. Put half of the onion rings on the baking sheet, then place them in the air fryer.

7. Cook for 8 to 12 minutes in an air fryer.

8. Repeat the process for the remaining ones.

9. Serve with sauce or as a side dish.

Cumin Baby Carrots

- **Servings:** 4 / **Prep Time:** 5 min / **Cook Time:** 20 min
- **Difficulty level:** Easy

Ingredients:

- *2 tbsp. of olive oil*
- *1-¼ lb. baby carrots*
- *½ tsp. of cumin powder*
- *1 tsp. of cumin seeds*
- *½ tsp. of garlic powder*
- *1 tsp. of salt*
- *½ tsp. of black pepper*
- *1 handful of cilantro, chopped*

Directions:

1. Preheat an air fryer to 370°F.

2. In a wide mixing bowl, place the carrots.

3. Add cumin powder, olive oil, cumin seeds, garlic powder, salt, and pepper, and mix well to coat.

4. Cook the baby carrots for 20 minutes in the basket of an air fryer.

5. Place on a serving platter and cover with minced cilantro.

Brussels Sprouts with Raisins

*****

- **Servings:** 4 / **Prep Time:** 5 min / **Cook Time:** 15 min
- **Difficulty level:** Easy

Ingredients:

- *2 oz. toasted pine nuts*
- *Juice and zest of 1 orange*
- *14 oz. Brussels sprouts, steamed*
- *1 tbsp. of olive oil*
- *2 oz. raisins*

Directions:

1. In the orange juice, soak raisins for about 20 minutes.

2. Preheat an air fryer to 370°F.

3. Sprinkle the Brussels sprouts with olive oil before placing them in the air fryer basket.

4. Cook for 15 minutes.

5. Serve with pine nuts, raisins, and orange zest in a dish.

Asparagus Fries

- **Servings:** 6 / **Prep Time:** 5 min / **Cook Time:** 16-20 min
- **Difficulty level:** Easy

Ingredients:

- *¼ cup of flour*
- *1 lb. asparagus spears*
- *½ cup of Parmesan cheese, grated*
- *1 cup of breadcrumbs*
- *Salt and pepper, to taste*
- *2 eggs, beaten*

Directions:

1. Preheat an air fryer to 370°F.

2. In a small mixing bowl, combine the Parmesan and breadcrumbs.

3. Season to taste with salt and pepper.

4. Line a baking sheet with parchment paper.

5. Coat half of the asparagus spears with flour, then dip them in eggs and then in breadcrumbs.

6. Put them on the baking sheet and bake for 8 to 10 minutes.

7. Do the same for the second half of the spears and serve it.

Zucchini Fries

- **Servings:** 4 / **Prep Time:** 10 min / **Cook Time:** 12 min / **Resting Time:** 10 min
- **Difficulty level:** Moderate

Ingredients:

Roasted Garlic Sauce:
- *2 tbsp. of Olive Oil*
- *1 tsp. of Roasted Garlic*
- *½ Cup of Mayonnaise*
- *Salt and Pepper*
- *Juice of ½ Lemon*

Zucchini Fries:
- *2 Eggs, Beaten*
- *½ Cup of Flour*
- *1 Cup of Seasoned Breadcrumbs*
- *Olive Oil Spray*
- *1 Large Zucchini, ½-Inch Sticks*
- *Salt and Pepper*

Directions:

1. Mix roasted garlic, olive oil, mayonnaise, and lemon juice in a bowl to make the sauce. Season the sauce with salt and pepper.

2. Then make zucchini fries. Use three shallow dishes. Season the flour well with grounded black pepper and salt in the first shallow dish. In the second shallow bowl, beat the eggs. Combine the salt, breadcrumbs, and pepper in the third shallow bowl. Coat zucchini sticks first with flour, then dip them in eggs and eventually toss them in breadcrumbs. Shake the

breadcrumbs into the dish and carefully sprinkle the crumbs on zucchini sticks to ensure equal coverage.

3. Spread the zucchini fries on a flat surface and set them aside for at least 10 mins before air frying to allow them to dry out. Preheat an air fryer at 400°F.

4. Coat zucchini sticks with olive oil and cook them in batches by placing them in single layers in the air-fryer basket. Cook the fries in the air fryer for 12 minutes, flipping and spinning halfway through. When you flip them over, spray them with more oil.

5. Toss zucchini fries with roasted garlic sauce and serve warm.

Ravioli

- **Servings:** 3 / **Prep Time:** 7 min / **Cook Time:** 6-8 min
- **Difficulty level:** Moderate

Ingredients:

- *1/4 cup of Parmesan cheese: shredded*
- *1 cup of breadcrumbs (seasoned)*
- *1/2 cup of flour (all-purpose)*
- *2 tsp. of dried basil*
- *1 package beef ravioli (9 ounces)*
- *2 lightly beaten large eggs*
- *Cooking spray*
- *1 cup of warmed marinara sauce*
- *Optional: Fresh minced basil*

Directions:

1. Preheat an air fryer to 350°F. Combine Parmesan cheese, breadcrumbs, and basil in a small dish. Mix flour and eggs into another small bowl. Coat all sides of ravioli with flour and shake off the waste. Dip in the eggs, then in the crumb mixture, patting down to adhere coating.

2. Place ravioli on a greased tray in the air-fryer basket, spritzed with cooking spray. Cook in batches for 3-4 minutes or until golden brown. Spray with cooking spray and switch. Cook for another 3-4 minutes, or until golden brown. Sprinkle basil and Parmesan cheese over it and serve it with marinara sauce.

Air Fryer Nuts and Bolts

*****

- **Servings:** 4 / **Prep Time:** 15 min / **Cook Time:** 15 min
- **Difficulty level:** Hard

Ingredients:
- *1/4 cup olive oil: extra virgin*
- *1 cup of Nutri-grain cereal*
- *2 cups of dried farfalle*
- *1 tsp. of onion powder*
- *1 tsp. of sea salt*
- *2 tbsp. of brown sugar*
- *1/2 tsp. of garlic powder*
- *2 teaspoons smoked paprika*
- *1/2 cup raw macadamias*
- *1/2 tsp. of chili powder*
- *1/2 cup raw cashews*
- *1 cup of pretzels*

Directions:

1. Cook pasta until tender in a wide saucepan with boiling salted water. Drain thoroughly. Place it on a tray. Use a paper towel, pat it dry and transfer to a wide mixing bowl.

2. In a small bowl, combine oil, sugar, paprika, garlic, onion, and chili powders. Half of the mixture is spooned over the pasta. Toss to uniformly coat it.

3. Preheat an air fryer to 392°F. In the air fryer basket, put the pasta (in tray or pan). For 5 minutes, cook it and shake the basket. For another 5-6 minutes, cook it, or until golden and crisp. Shift it to a wide mixing bowl.

4. Add pretzels and nuts and combine them well. Add the rest of the spice mix. Toss to uniformly coat. Transfer it to the basket of an air fryer. Cook for 3 minutes at 356°F. Shake basket. Cook for an extra 2-3 minutes, or until golden brown. Add it to pasta and toss in the cereal. Season with salt. Mix well. Let it cool and serve it.

Chapter 4: Vegetarian Recipes

Cabbage Steaks

*****

- **Servings:** 3 / **Prep Time:** 5 min / **Cook Time:** 15 min
- **Difficulty level:** Easy

Ingredients:

- *2 tbsp. of olive oil*
- *1 cabbage head*
- *½ tsp. of black pepper*
- *1 tbsp. of garlic paste*
- *2 tsp. of fennel seeds*
- *1 tsp. of salt*

Directions:

1. Preheat an air fryer to 350°F.

2. Cut the cabbage into 1- to 12-inch-thick strips.

3. Combine all remaining ingredients in a shallow bowl.

4. Add the mixture to the cabbage.

5. In your air fryer, arrange the cabbage steaks and cook for 15 minutes and then serve them.

Pasta with Roasted Veggies

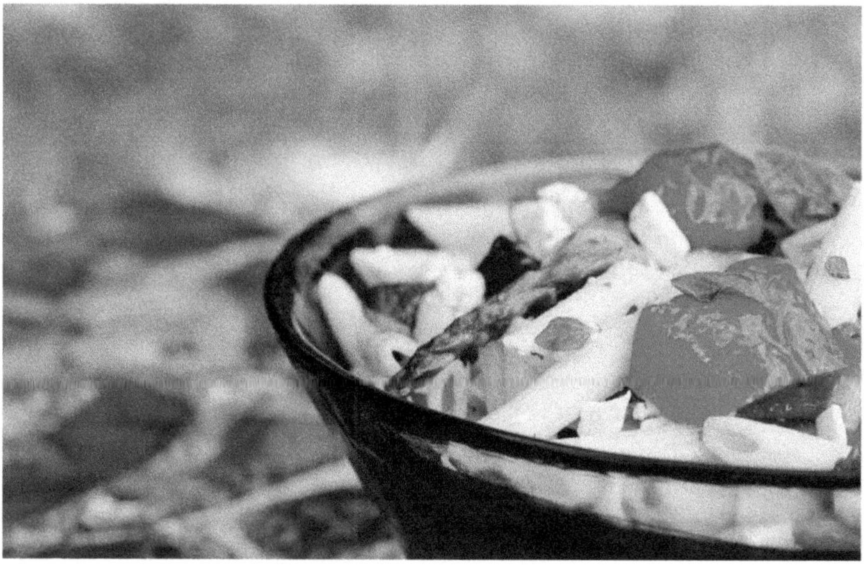

- **Servings:** 6 / **Prep Time:** 15 min / **Cook Time:** 15 min
- **Difficulty level:** Moderate

Ingredients:
- *4 oz. Mushrooms, sliced*
- *1 lb. cooked penne*
- *½ cup of pitted and halved kalamata olives*
- *1 zucchini, sliced*
- *¼ cup of olive oil*
- *1 pepper, sliced*
- *3 tbsp. of balsamic vinegar*
- *1 acorn squash, sliced*
- *2 tbsp. of chopped basil*
- *1 tsp. of Italian seasoning*
- *Salt and pepper, to taste*
- *1 cup of grape tomatoes, halved.*

Directions:

1. Preheat an air fryer to 380°F.

2. In a big mixing bowl, combine the zucchini, pepper, mushrooms, squash, and olive oil.

3. Season to taste with salt and pepper.

4. Cook the vegetables for 15 minutes in the air fryer.

5. Mix the roasted vegetables, penne, olives, Italian seasoning, tomatoes, and vinegar in a wide bowl.

6. Divide them among 6 serving bowls and cover with basil.

Spicy Pepper, Sweet Potato Skewers

*****

- **Servings:** 1 / **Prep Time:** 10 min / **Cook Time:** 15 min
- **Difficulty level:** Moderate

Ingredients:
- ¼ tsp. of black pepper
- 1 large sweet potato
- ½ tsp. of turmeric
- 1 beetroot
- 1 tbsp. of olive oil
- ¼ tsp. of garlic powder
- 1 green bell pepper
- ¼ tsp. of paprika
- 1 tsp. of chili flakes

Directions:

1. Soak 3 to 4 skewers.

2. Preheat an air fryer to 350°F.

3. Peel and cut the vegetables into chunks.

4. Combine the chunks and the other ingredients in a mixing bowl. Toss until it is uniformly coated.

5. Assemble the vegetables in the following manner on a skewer: potato, pepper, and beetroot. Place in the air fryer for 15 minutes, cook it and then serve it.

Quinoa and Veggie Stuffed Peppers

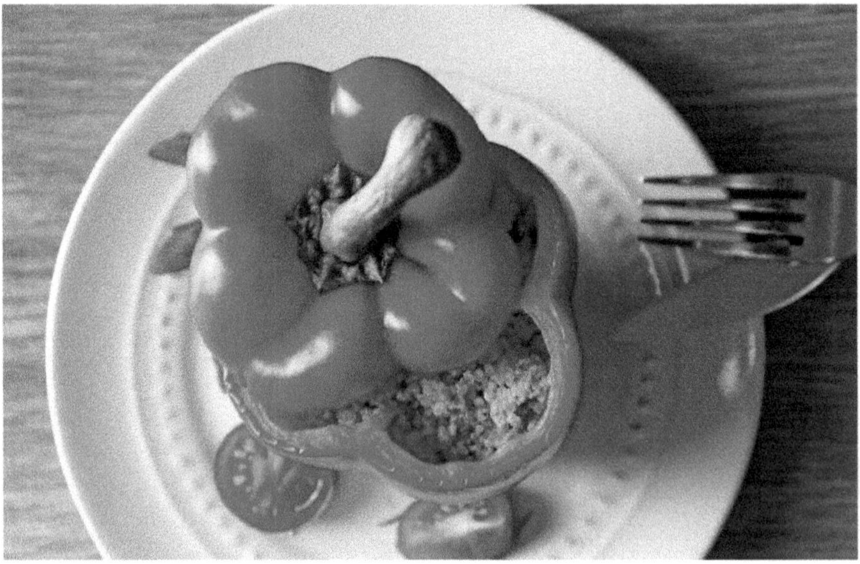

- **Servings:** 1 / **Prep Time:** 6 min / **Cook Time:** 10 min
- **Difficulty level:** Moderate

Ingredients:

- *½ diced tomato*
- *¼ cup of cooked quinoa*
- *½ tbsp. of diced onion*
- *1 bell pepper*
- *Salt and pepper, to taste*
- *¼ tsp. of smoked paprika*
- *¼ tsp. of dried basil*
- *1 tsp. of olive oil*

Directions:

1. Preheat an air fryer to 350°F.

2. To prepare the bell pepper for the stuffing, clean it and cut off the top, which will serve as the lid.

3. Brush half of the olive oil on the outside of the pepper.

4. Blend remaining ingredients in a small bowl, except half-teaspoon olive oil.

5. Fill the pepper with the stuffing.

6. Cover with the top of the bell pepper.

7. Drizzle the remaining half-teaspoon of olive oil and sprinkle with the basil.

8. Cook for 10 minutes in an air fryer.

Veggie Kebab

- **Servings:** 4 / **Prep Time:** 10 min / **Cook Time:** 10 min
- **Difficulty level:** Moderate

Ingredients:

- *2 tbsp. of corn flour*
- *2/3 cup of canned beans*
- *1/3 cup of grated carrots*
- *Two boiled plus mashed potatoes*
- *¼ cup of fresh mint leaves: chopped*
- *½ tsp. of garam masala powder*
- *½ cup of paneer*
- *Fresh ginger: 1-inch piece*
- *1 green chili*
- *Salt, to taste*
- *3 garlic cloves*

Directions:

1. Before using soak 12 skewers

2. Set an air fryer to 390°F.

3. In a food processor, blend carrots, paneer, beans, garlic, chili, ginger, and mint until smooth. Put in a mixing dish.

4. Combine the corn flour, mashed potatoes, salt, and garam masala powder in a bowl.

5. Stir until it is well combined.

6. Divide the mixture into 12 equal parts.

7. Wrap them around a skewer. Cook in the air for 10 minutes and serve it warm.

Potato Filled Bread Rolls

- **Servings:** 4 / **Prep Time:** 10 min / **Cook Time:** 17 min
- **Difficulty level:** Moderate

Ingredients:

- *5 large boiled and mashed potatoes*
- *8 slices of bread*
- *Salt, to taste*
- *½ tsp. of turmeric*
- *2 deseeded and chopped green chilies*
- *1 tbsp. of olive oil*
- *1 medium finely chopped onion*
- *2 sprigs curry leaf*
- *½ tsp. of mustard seeds*

Directions:

1. Preheat an air fryer to 350°F.

2. On a baking tray, combine the onion, olive oil, mustard seed, and curry leaves.mCook for 5 minutes in an air fryer.

3. Combine the onion paste with chilies, mashed potatoes, turmeric, and salt in a mixing bowl. Divide the mixture into 8 equal portions.

4. Trim the bread's edges and moist it with water. Ensure that excess water is drained.

5. The potato mixture is placed in the middle of one wet bread slice. Seal the sides of the bread by rolling it over the filling.

6. Place the rolls in a baking dish lined with parchment paper and air fry it for 12 minutes.

Roasted Green Beans

*****

- **Servings:** 6/ **Prep Time:** 7 min / **Cook Time:** 16-20 min
- **Difficulty level:** Easy

Ingredients:

- *1/2 pound of sliced mushrooms (fresh)*
- *1-pound green beans (fresh) Sliced into 2-inch pieces*
- *2 tbsp. of olive oil*
- *1 small thinly sliced red onion*
- *1 tsp. of Italian seasoning*
- *1/8 tsp. of pepper*
- *Salt to taste*

Directions:

1. Preheat an air fryer to 375°F. Mix all ingredients in a wide mixing bowl and toss to coat them.

2. Place vegetables in an air-fryer basket on a greased tray.

3. For 8-10 minutes, cook it, or until just tender.

4. Stir to redistribute; cook for another 8-10 minutes, or until browned.

Chapter 5: Fish and Seafood Recipes

Crab Cakes

- **Servings:** 4 / **Prep Time:** 10 min / **Cook Time:** 7 min / **Resting Time:** 30 min
- **Difficulty level:** Moderate

Ingredients:
- *Cooking spray*
- *½ cup cooked crab meat*
- *1 tbsp. of chopped basil*
- *¼ cup of chopped celery*
- *3 tbsp. of mayonnaise*
- *¼ cup of chopped red pepper*
- *¼ cup of breadcrumbs*
- *Zest of half a lemon*
- *2 tbsp. of chopped parsley*
- *Bay seasoning, as desired*
- *¼ cup of chopped red onion*

Directions:

1. Heat an air fryer to 390°F.

2. In a wide mixing bowl, combine all the ingredients and stir well until thoroughly combined.

3. Shape the mixture into four large crab cakes and arrange them on a parchment-lined baking sheet.

4. Refrigerate for 30 minutes to enable flavors to set.

5. Coat the air basket with cooking spray and fill it with crab cakes.

6. Cook each side for around 7 minutes, then serve it warm.

Cajun Lemony Salmon

*****

- **Servings:** 1 / **Prep Time:** 5 min / **Cook Time:** 7-9 min
- **Difficulty level:** Easy

Ingredients:
- *1 tbsp. of chopped parsley for garnishing*
- *Juice of ½ lemon*
- *1 tbsp. of Cajun seasoning*
- *1 salmon fillet*
- *¼ tsp. of brown sugar*
- *2 lemon wedges; for serving*

Directions:

1. Preheat an air fryer to 350°F.

2. In the meantime, combine the lemon juice and sugar and cover the salmon fully.

3. Season the salmon with Cajun seasoning.

4. Place it on parchment paper in your air fryer and cook for 7 minutes (Cook for no more than 6 minutes if using a thinner fillet).

5. Garnish with lemon wedges and parsley.

Cod Cornflakes Nuggets

✶✶✶✶✶

- **Servings:** 4 / **Prep Time:** 7 min / **Cook Time:** 15 min
- **Difficulty level:** Moderate

Ingredients:

- *½ cup of flour*
- *1-¼ lb. cod fillets divided into 4 to 6 chunks*
- *1 egg*
- *salt, and pepper, to taste*
- *1 tbsp. of water*
- *1 tbsp. of olive oil*
- *1 cup of cornflakes (use more if required)*

Directions:

1. In a food processor, blend the oil and cornflakes and process them until crumbed.

2. Sprinkle salt and pepper over the fish chunks.

3. In a mixing bowl, mix egg and 1 tablespoon of water.

4. First, dredge the chunks in flour, then dip them in the egg, and finally cover them in cornflakes.

5. Arrange the pieces on a lined sheet.

6. For 15 minutes, air fry them at 350 ° F.

7. Serve it once done.

Tuna Patties

*****

- **Servings:** 2 / **Prep Time:** 7 min / **Cook Time:** 12 min / **Resting Time:** 30 min
- **Difficulty level:** Moderate

Ingredients:

- *1 tsp. of lime juice*
- *5 oz. of canned tuna*
- *1 tsp. of paprika*
- *¼ of cup flour*
- *1 tsp. of chili powder, optional*
- *2 eggs*
- *1 small onion, diced*
- *½ of cup milk*
- *½ tsp. of salt*

Directions:

1. In a mixing bowl, mix all ingredients and stir well to combine.

2. Shape the mixture into two big patties or a few smaller patties.

3. Refrigerate for 30 minutes after placing them on a lined baking sheet.

4. Preheat an air fryer to 350° F.

5. Cook the patties for around 6 minutes on each side in an air fryer.

Pistachio Crusted Salmon

*****

- **Servings:** 1 / **Prep Time:** 10 min / **Cook Time:** 10 min
- **Difficulty level:** Easy

Ingredients:

- *3 tbsp. of pistachios*
- *1 tsp. of olive oil*
- *One salmon fillet*
- *Pinch of sea salt*
- *1 tsp. of mustard*
- *Pinch of garlic powder*
- *1 tsp. of lemon juice*
- *Pinch of black pepper*
- *1 tsp. of Parmesan cheese; grated*

Directions:

1. An air fryer is preheated to 350° F.

2. Mix mustard and lemon juice in a mixing bowl.

3. Coat salmon with pepper, salt, and garlic powder.

4. Brush both sides with olive oil.

5. Then coat salmon with the mustard/lemon combination.

6. Finely chop the pistachios and mix them with the Parmesan cheese. Cover salmon with it and coat well.

7. Put the salmon in the air fryer basket with the skin-side down.

8. Cook for 10 minutes or until done.

Chapter 6: Poultry and Beef Recipes

Southern Drumsticks

- **Servings:** 4 / **Prep Time:** 10 min / **Cook Time:** 40 min
- **Difficulty level:** Moderate

Ingredients:

- *2 tbsp. of thyme*
- *8 chicken drumsticks*
- *2 tbsp. of oregano*
- *¼ cup of milk*
- *2 oz. Oats*
- *¼ steamed cauliflower florets*
- *1 egg*
- *Salt and pepper, to taste*
- *1 tsp. of ground cayenne*

Directions:

1. Preheat an air fryer to 350°F.

2. Sprinkle salt and pepper on the drumsticks.

3. Use the milk to coat them.

4. In a food processor, combine all the remaining ingredients, except the egg.

5. Blend until fully smooth.

6. Start by dipping each drumstick in the egg, then in the oat mixture. Place half of them inside the air fryer on a baking mat/pan.

7. Cook for 20 minutes at 350°F.

8. Do the same for the next batch and serve them hot.

Rosemary Lemon Chicken

*****

- **Servings:** 2 / **Prep Time:** 10 min / **Cook Time:** 20 min / **Resting Time:** 30 min
- **Difficulty level:** Moderate

Ingredients:

- *1 tsp. of minced ginger*
- *2 chicken breasts*
- *½ lemon, wedges*
- *2 rosemary sprigs*
- *½ tbsp. of olive oil*
- *1 tbsp. of soy sauce*
- *3 tbsp. of brown sugar*
- *1 tbsp. of oyster sauce*

Directions:

1. Combine the ginger, soy sauce, and olive oil in a small bowl. Toss in the chicken and cover thoroughly.

2. Refrigerate the bowl for 30 minutes after covering it.

3. Preheat an air fryer to 370°F.

4. Place the marinated chicken in an oven-safe baking dish and then into an air fryer. For about 6 minutes, cook it.

5. In a shallow dish, combine rosemary, oyster sauce, and brown sugar. Drizzle the sauce on top of the chicken.

6. Place the lemon wedges in the serving dish.

7. Cook for another 13 minutes in the air fryer and serve it.

Panko Turkey

- **Servings:** 6 / **Prep Time:** 10 min / **Cook Time:** 8-15 min
- **Difficulty level:** Moderate

Ingredients:
- *1 tsp. of salt*
- *2 cups of panko*
- *6 turkey breasts, skinless and boneless*
- *½ tsp. of cayenne pepper*
- *1 stick butter, melted*
- *½ tsp. of black pepper*

Directions:

1. Toss the panko with half of the cayenne pepper, black pepper, and salt in a mixing bowl.

2. Combine the salt, melted butter, and pepper in a separate small dish.

3. If you're using salted butter, cut out the salt.

4. Coat turkey with the butter mixture.

5. Use the panko paste to coat the turkey.

6. On a lined baking dish, arrange them.

7. Preheat an air fryer to 390°F and air fry for 15 minutes.

8. Cook for 8 minutes if the turkey breasts are thinner. Serve it warm.

Crumbed Sage Chicken Scallopini

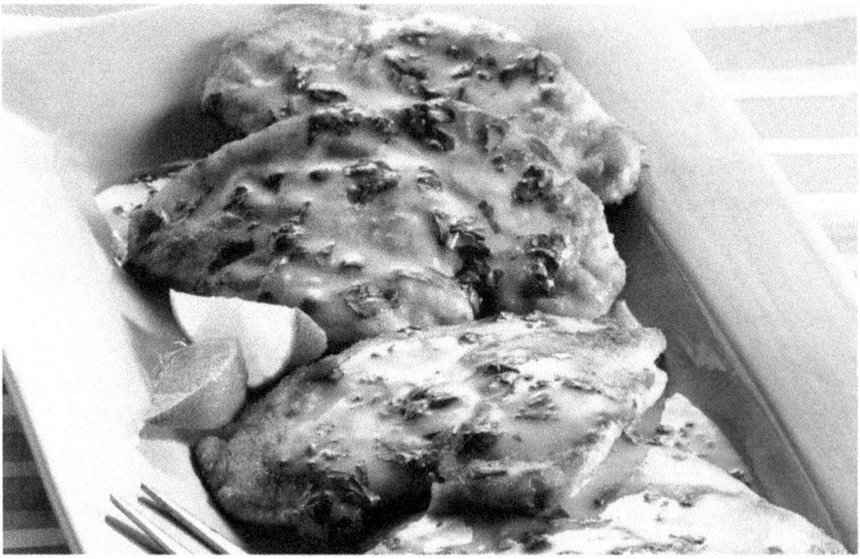

- **Servings:** 4 / **Prep Time:** 7 min / **Cook Time:** 7 min
- **Difficulty level:** Moderate

Ingredients:

- *4 chicken breasts, skinless and boneless*
- *Cooking spray*
- *2 eggs, beaten*
- *Breadcrumbs*
- *1 tbsp. of fresh, chopped sage*
- *2 oz. flour*
- *2 tbsp. of grated Parmesan cheese*

Directions:

1. Preheat an air fryer to 370°F.

2. Cover the chicken breasts with plastic wrap from underneath and on top.

3. Roll out the meat with a rolling pin until it is very thin.

4. Toss the sage, Parmesan, and breadcrumbs together in a shallow dish.

5. Dip the chicken first in the egg, then in the sage combination.

6. Spray the meat with cooking oil and place it in the air fryer.

7. For about 7 minutes, cook it and serve it.

Sweet Garlicky Chicken Wings

- **Servings:** 4 / **Prep Time:** 5 min / **Cook Time:** 15 min
- **Difficulty level:** Moderate

Ingredients:
- ¼ cup of butter
- 16 chicken wings
- ½ tsp. of salt
- ¼ cup of honey
- ¾ cup of potato starch
- 4 garlic cloves, minced

Directions:

1. Preheat an air fryer to 370°F.

2. Put the wings in a bowl after rinsing and patting them dry.

3. Toss the chicken in the starch and toss to cover.

4. Chicken is assembled in a baking dish that has been finely covered with cooking oil.

5. Cook for 5 minutes.

6. In a separate dish, mix the remaining ingredients.

7. Cook for another 10 minutes after pouring the sauce over the wings and enjoy it.

Panko Beef Schnitzel

- **Servings:** 1 / **Prep Time:** 10 min / **Cook Time:** 12 min
- **Difficulty level:** Moderate

Ingredients:

- *1 thin beef cutlet*
- *2 tbsp. of olive oil*
- *1 tsp. of paprika*
- *Salt and pepper, to taste*
- *1 egg, beaten*
- *¼ tsp. of garlic powder*
- *2 oz. breadcrumbs*

Directions:

1. Preheat an air fryer to 350°F.

2. In a large mixing bowl, combine the breadcrumbs, olive oil, paprika, salt, and garlic powder.

3. Dip the beef in the egg first, then fully cover it in the breadcrumb mixture.

4. Put the breaded meat in a baking dish/pan lined with parchment paper.

5. For about 12 minutes, cook it and serve it.

Beef Bulgogi

*****

- **Servings:** 1 / **Prep Time:** 15 min / **Cook Time:** 10 min / **Resting Time:** 3 hours
- **Difficulty level:** Moderate

Ingredients:

- *1 tbsp. of diced onion*
- *6 oz. beef*
- *2 tbsp. of bulgogi marinade*
- *½ cup of sliced mushrooms*

Directions:

1. Place the beef in a bowl and cut it into small sections.

2. Toss in the bulgogi and thoroughly cover the meat.

3. To marinate, cover the bowl and put it in the fridge for around 3 hours.

4. Preheat an air fryer to 350°F.

5. Place the beef in a baking dish/pan. Add the mushroom and onion and mix well.

6. Cook for about 10 minutes.

7. Enjoy it with a green salad and roasted potatoes.

Thai Roasted Beef

****

- **Servings:** 2-3 / **Prep Time:** 10 min / **Cook Time:** 12 min / **Resting Time:** 4 hours
- **Difficulty level:** Moderate

Ingredients:
- 2 tbsp. of soy sauce
- 1 lb. ground beef
- 2 tbsp. of basil, chopped
- Thumb-sized piece of ginger, chopped
- 2 tbsp. of mirin
- ½ tsp. of salt
- 3 chilies deseeded and chopped
- 2 tbsp. of coriander, chopped
- ½ tsp. of pepper
- 2 tbsp. of oil
- 4 garlic cloves, chopped
- 2 tbsp. of fish sauce
- Juice of 1 lime
- 1 tsp. of brown sugar

Directions:

1. Combine all the ingredients in the processor except the salt, beef, and pepper. Blend until fully smooth.

2. Sprinkle pepper and salt over the beef and place it in a zipper bag. Shake it so that beef marinates well, set it aside for a while. Then add all ingredients to a large mixing bowl including beef and set aside to marinate in the refrigerator for 4 hours.

3. Set an air fryer to 350°F. Cook the beef in the air fryer for around 12 minutes or longer if you like it well cooked. Allow to set it for a few minutes before serving.

Chapter 7: Dessert Recipes

White Filling Coconut and Oat Cookies

*****

- **Servings:** 4 / **Prep Time:** 12 min / **Cook Time:** 18 min
- **Difficulty level:** Moderate

Ingredients:
- ¼ cup of coconut flakes
- 1/3 cup of butter
- 5-½ oz. flour
- 3 oz. sugar
- 1 tsp. of vanilla extract
- 1 small egg, beaten
- ½ cup of oats

Filling:
- 4 oz. powdered sugar
- 1 oz. White chocolate, melted
- 1 tsp. of vanilla extract
- 2 oz. butter

Directions:

1. Use an electric mixer to combine all cookie ingredients except the flour.

2. Add in the flour until the mixture is smooth.

3. Pour a spoonful of batter onto a baking sheet lined with parchment paper.

4. Cook for 18 minutes in an air fryer at 350° F. Allow cooling.

5. Make the filling by blending all ingredients.

6. Spread filling on cookies. To make cookie sandwiches, top with the remaining halves.

Molten Lava Cake

- **Servings:** 4 / **Prep Time:** 10 min / **Cook Time:** 10 min
- **Difficulty level:** Moderate

Ingredients:
- *1-½ tbsp. of self-rising flour*
- *3-½ oz. Butter, melted*
- *2 eggs*
- *3-½ tbsp. of sugar*
- *3-½ oz. Dark chocolate, melted*

Directions:

1. Brush melted butter on four ramekins and preheat an air fryer to 375° F.

2. Blend eggs and sugar until frothy.

3. Then add the chocolate and butter into the same mixing bowl.

4. Add in the flour gently.

5. Pour mixture into ramekins and bake for 10 minutes in the air fryer.

6. Allow the lava cakes to cool for 2 minutes before turning them upside down onto serving plates.

Candied Bananas

$$*****$$

- **Servings:** 1 / **Prep Time:** 5 min / **Cook Time:** 6-8 min
- **Difficulty level:** Moderate

Ingredients:

- *1/4 of lemon; juiced*
- *2 bananas*
- *Optional toppings: nuts, cinnamon, coconut cream, granola, yogurt, etc.*
- *1 tbsp of coconut sugar*

Directions:

1. Wash bananas with peel, then cut them lengthwise down the center.

2. Drizzle lemon juice over each banana.

3. Combine the coconut sugar and cinnamon, then scatter over the bananas until evenly covered.

4. Cook for 6-8 minutes at 400°F in an air fryer lined with parchment paper.

5. Serve simple or with your favorite toppings immediately after removing from the air fryer.

Apple Pie

- **Servings:** 9 / **Prep Time:** 10 min / **Cook Time:** 20 min
- **Difficulty level:** Moderate

Ingredients:

- *2 oz. sugar*
- *4 apples, diced*
- *1 oz. brown sugar*
- *2 oz. butter, melted*
- *1 egg, beaten*
- *2 tsp. of cinnamon*
- *¼ tsp. of salt*
- *3 large puff pastry sheets*

Directions:

1. In a mixing bowl, combine the brown sugar, white sugar, cinnamon, butter, and salt.

2. Coat the apples in the mixture and place them in a baking dish.

3. Preheat the air fryer to 350° F and cook for 10 minutes.

4. Meanwhile, on a floured level surface, roll out the puff pastry and split each sheet into 6 equal parts. Cover the pieces with the apple filling.

5. Brush the egg mixture on the edges of the pastry squares. Fold them and use a fork to close the ends.

6. Arrange on a lined baking sheet and cook for 8 minutes in the air fryer at 350° F.

7. Flip them over, raise the temperature to 390°F, and cook for an additional 2 minutes. Serve it.

Orange Sponge Cake

- **Servings:** 6 / **Prep Time:** 15 min / **Cook Time:** 30 min
- **Difficulty level:** Moderate

Ingredients:
- *1 tsp. of baking powder*
- *9 oz. self-rising flour*
- *3 eggs*
- *9 oz. butter*
- *Zest of 1 orange*
- *9 oz. sugar*
- *1 tsp. of vanilla extract*

Frosting:
- *7 oz. superfine sugar*
- *4 egg whites*
- *1 tsp. of orange food coloring*
- *Zest of 1 orange*
- *Juice of 1 orange*

Directions:

1. Heat the air fryer to 160°F.

2. In a mixing bowl, combine cake ingredients and beat with an electric mixer until smooth.

3. Pour half of the batter into a cake pan that has been lined with parchment paper and bake for 15 minutes in an air fryer. Repeat the same with the remaining batter.

4. In the meantime, make the frosting by fusing together all the frosting ingredients.

5. Cover one cake with frosting and place the other cake on top. Enjoy it at teatime.

Mock Cherry Pie

$$*****$$

- **Servings:** 8 / **Prep Time:** 15 min / **Cook Time:** 20 min
- **Difficulty level:** Moderate

Ingredients:

- *1 tbsp. of milk*
- *2 pie crusts; store-bought*
- *1 egg yolk*
- *21 oz. cherry pie filling*

Directions:

1. Preheat an air fryer to 310°F.

2. In a pie pan, arrange one piecrust.

3. Make holes with a fork in the crust and bake it for 5 minutes.

4. Add the pie filling on top.

5. Split the remaining pie crust into strips and lay them over the baked crust in a pie-style pattern.

6. Mix egg yolk and milk in a bowl and brush it over the pie.

7. Place the pie back in the air fryer and bake for another 15 minutes.

Simple Coffee Cake

- **Servings:** 2 / **Prep Time:** 10 min / **Cook Time:** 15 min
- **Difficulty level:** Moderate

Ingredients:
- *1 egg*
- *¼ cup of butter*
- *1 tbsp. of black coffee, brewed*
- *½ tsp. of instant coffee*
- *¼ cup of sugar*
- *1 tsp. of cocoa powder*
- *¼ cup of flour*
- *Powdered sugar for icing*
- *Pinch of salt*

Directions:

1. Heat an air fryer to 330°F.

2. Grease a small round cake pan.

3. In a mixing dish, combine the sugar and egg.

4. Add cocoa, instant coffee, and black coffee.

5. Mix in the flour and salt.

6. Pour the batter into the pan that has been prepared.

7. Bake for 15 minutes and serve it.

Baked apples

*****

- **Servings:** 2 / **Prep Time:** 5 min / **Cook Time:** 10 min
- **Difficulty level:** Moderate

Ingredients:
- *2 tbsp. of brown sugar*
- *4 apples*
- *2 oz. breadcrumbs*
- *1 oz. butter*
- *2 oz. mixed seeds by choice*
- *Zest of 1 orange*
- *1 tsp. of cinnamon*
- *2 tbsp. of chopped hazelnuts for garnish*

Directions:

1. Heat the air fryer to 350°F.

2. Peel apples to avoid them from splitting and core them.

3. In a mixing bowl, combine the remaining ingredients.

4. Coat the apples with the mixture and bake them for 10 minutes in an air fryer.

5. Garnish with chopped hazelnuts.

Conclusion

Cooking is a creative endeavor, and following recipes is just the start. The multi-functional Air Fryer is designed to help you get started in the cooking journey. To do it successfully, you must first understand all the functions and options available to you with this wonderful kitchen assistant. Vortex employs smart programming to help you air fry, bake, and cook at the correct temperature and time. The programming is easy and basic, guiding you through the whole cooking phase. It advises you when to add the food, shuffles the cooking tray, and taking it out. Because of its fast air circulation operation, the Air Fryer requires little or no oil to cook or bake food.

The Air Fryer is specifically intended to make cooking easy for those who live stressful schedules and do not want to sacrifice over delicious foods. It can, however, be used for more complex and involving recipes since it is a completely functional appliance depending on the level of enthusiasm for cooking. When you begin to use your fryer more frequently for easy, fast, tasty, and filling meals, this beginner's book will come in handy. Each person's palate and taste preferences are unique.

You may make changes to these recipes if required. Get to know how the recipes work and what changes you might bring to them.

You will need to vary the cook times and temperatures with different changes to the recipes, which will improve your kitchen skills and your ability to use your Air Fryer.

You can use your Air Fryer to create breakfast, lunch, meals, and desserts, just as you did for the recipes in this book. It may also be used for sandwiches, appetizers, and side dishes to complete any well-rounded meal. This book has all the recipes you'll ever need. Best of luck with your cooking adventures.

Lightning Source UK Ltd.
Milton Keynes UK
UKHW020658310521
384668UK00001B/67

9 781802 349436